For our earth's most precious
resource: our children

This book was sponsored by generous contributions from:

Sayma Rahman and Faisal Hossain

University of Washington

Gordon and Betty Moore Foundation

The idea for this children's book was conceived in 2018 as part of a program called the New Voices under the National Academies of Science, Engineering, and Medicine. In my lifelong passion for science communication, I toyed with the idea of using fun, cartoon illustrations to describe inspirational and hopeful stories about extraordinary scientists, engineers, and doctors. By highlighting a personal story of struggle, a moment, or a journey, my hope was that our children will understand that they, too, can become successful professionals in science, medicine, engineering, and other allied disciplines. The purpose of the idea was to show our children that, while pursuing such disciplines, it is still okay to fail or be different from others, because all successful scientists, doctors, and engineers were just like them once. So in early 2019, the journey to publish this book for elementary school-aged children began.

I want to thank two particular New Voices members who went above and beyond in accompanying me on this journey: Colleen Iversen and Tyrone Grandison. Together, Tyrone and Colleen built the apparatus for the dissemination and collection of stories, and cheered us on with their common passion for selfless service to others. This book could not have been completed without the sacrifices Tyrone and Colleen made this past year. I also want to thank the New Voices initial cohort of 2018 who allowed their stories to be used to prototype such an effort. Last but not least, I am very grateful to the sustained and affordable illustrator services provided by my dear friends Merve Cirisoglu and Hatice Sena Balkan of Animatick Arts. If it were not for their willingness to patiently listen to me and other authors' visual wish lists, this book would never have been published with the very limited resources we had.

So, after two years of relentless effort, I am now pleased to share this book with our earth's most precious resources—our children. I hope they like it, because we are just getting started!

Faisal Hossain
Bothell, Washington

www.mascotbooks.com

The Secret Lives of Scientists, Engineers, and Doctors: Volume 1

Illustration artwork by Hatice Sena Balkan and illustration design by
Merve Cirisoglu of Animatick Arts; animatick.com.

For more information, please contact:
Mascot Books
620 Herndon Parkway, Suite 320
Herndon, VA 20170
info@mascotbooks.com

Library of Congress Control Number: 2020912682

CPSIA Code: PRT0820A
ISBN-13: 978-1-64543-445-0

Printed in the United States

The
Secret Lives
of
Scientists,
Engineers,
and Doctors

Volume 1

Faisal Hossain

Illustrated by Hatice Sena Balkan
and Merve Cirisoglu

Ousman Mahmud

IBM Watson Health

As a child, I was always an inquisitive individual, full of curiosity and dedicated to my education. Imagine wading in knee-deep waters or being stacked in buses like sardines in a can just to achieve a goal. These were some of my experiences while pursuing elementary school education in The Gambia, where I was born and raised. When I learned how much preventable diseases contribute to the death of many people in The Gambia, I decided to pursue biomedical research. My doctoral research on malaria-causing pathogens really hit home because malaria is a huge problem in The Gambia.

To pursue my college education and graduate school, I had to leave everything behind in The Gambia and immigrate to the United States. This change is still the greatest challenge I have ever faced, but it also led to my greatest achievements, including getting a PhD in genetics. As an immigrant, I experienced culture shock, since The Gambia and the United States are very different. I had trouble navigating the "unknowns"—the little decisions that can change someone's life. I grappled with imposter syndrome—that tiny voice questioning if I'm good enough, even though I know I am. But imagine being the only black person at a conference of over 300 people, or the only black person at your workplace.

These experiences throughout my journey have led me to become an advocate for broadening the participation of underrepresented groups in the fields of science, technology, engineering, and mathematics (STEM). I have started Scientists of The Gambia, a social media initiative which seeks to inspire young Gambians to pursue STEM careers. I hope that by engaging in these activities, I can inspire those from underrepresented groups to pursue STEM careers.

Jorge Luiz Mazza Rodrigues

University of California, Davis

Jorge Luiz Mazza Rodrigues is a detective working in the Amazon rainforest trying to discover how microbes respond to the threat of deforestation. Growing up, he was always fascinated by the diversity of biological "things," such as numerous plant and animal species sharing and competing for resources. Now multiply the number of plants and animals by hundreds, and you have the number of microbes living in soils. These microorganisms have an enormous impact on our planet by controlling biogeochemical cycles, helping to clean up toxic spills, and providing us with delicious foods and biotechnological products that save lives. Likewise, humans have had a great impact on earth by changing the surface of our planet at a very fast pace for the last 150 years. How these man-made alterations affect microbes and what the consequences are of these alterations to our planet is what Jorge is investigating.

Inside the forest, sometimes Jorge walks for hours just to collect soils and bring them back with him. These soil samples hold information on thousands of microbial species, their genetic makeup, and what happens when humans destroy the Amazon rainforest. While some microbes go extinct, other microbes may take over, altering the nutrient cycles that plants and animals depend on in order to grow. He interrogates the soil for clues about microbes that have vanished, collects evidence, and records his investigation on the conversion of the Amazon rainforest into pastures. This detective story is just beginning, and it is time to search for other clues inside the forest.

Christopher Steven Marcum

The National Institutes of Health

The high school I attended—called Telstar, after the first television broadcast satellite—had some really cool classes. After taking forensic chemistry my junior year, I thought I wanted to be a toxicologist or entomologist (someone who studies insects) to help solve crimes with science. Then, in the fall of my senior year, I took two electives that changed all that: "Probability through Gaming" and "Introduction to Social Problems." I gained a basic knowledge of statistics through the gaming course, as we learned about odds and probability distributions by playing cards. The questions that interested me began to change. How are crimes committed? What are the social conditions under which people come to commit crimes? How is society organized in general? My high school social studies teacher (hi, Ray!) suggested that my interest in social problems might make me a good future sociologist and encouraged me to study society with maths. So, that's what I did.

Fast-forward twenty years, after earning a BA in sociology, an MA in demography, and a PhD in sociology, I'm now a scientist at the very prestigious National Institutes of Health. I study how social processes and social networks influence health, and how that dynamic changes as people age. I'm really interested in how social networks can be used to improve human health and well-being and also how health, in turn, shapes how society is organized into social networks. My job lets me invent methods and tools that other people can use in their research. My job is also about training the next generation of excellent STEM (science, technology, engineering, and math) scholars. I feel rewarded because as a mentor, I get to train the next generation to be future physicians, mathematicians, psychologists, geneticists, and even, occasionally, future sociologists.

Heidi Steltzer

Fort Lewis College

A just world. An equal world. A sustainable world. All these are possible. This is my purpose, a long journey I have only recently understood. I am an environmental scientist and explorer, seeking opportunities to go places others don't. I conduct research in the mountains and Arctic—regions of our planet where climate is rapidly changing.

Why go where others don't? To challenge myself. To escape. To be somewhere anything is possible, even an unlikely demise. To bear witness to our changing earth.

Half my life ago, the mountains and Arctic became my home. On a whim, I decided to spend a summer living at a remote field station in Colorado, the Rocky Mountain Biological Laboratory, and conducted research on a distant mountain hillslope. I was twenty-one years old and had rarely camped. I dared myself to spend days, and some nights, alone in green mountain meadows. I felt protected by the plants that surrounded me.

Five years later, I'd lived for many summers in a mountain cabin, hiked miles above tree line alone, and earned my PhD. I chose to study alpine tundra ecosystems. I wanted science to influence policy and thought this would require political reform.

Pursuing a career in science has not been simple. I'm not competitive; power is not important to me. I felt constrained by the expected behaviors and available choices. As a woman and a leader, the path to achievement in science was not clear.

I've been exploring earth for over twenty years. I want to share stories about its beauty and its strength, its vulnerability and my own. I want to hear others' tales of discovery and concern and identify common ground. Together, we can foster greater security for all. For a sustainable world, we must protect ourselves.

Carl G. Streed Jr.
Boston University

Feeling ill with flu-like symptoms and swollen lymph nodes in college, I dragged myself to see the campus doctor. I recall telling the doctor about my fever, my final exams, and about being stressed out. Then I mentioned my boyfriend.

The previously comforting doctor got very cold and brusque. As soon as I revealed myself to be gay, she said, "You really have to get an HIV test." I wasn't out to my parents at that time, but I was on their health insurance, so I couldn't get the test that way. I asked, "What else can I do?" She curtly said, "I don't know." She left the room and never came back.

I was furious. How could a doctor abandon their patient? I avoided doctors for a long time after that. I had to go to my hometown county health department to find free HIV testing and do it in secret without telling my parents. My motivation for becoming a doctor was that bad experience.

Now, as a professor of medicine and research lead at Boston University School of Medicine, I dedicate some of my time to assessing and educating physicians on how to better care for sexual and gender minorities (i.e., lesbian, gay, bisexual, transgender, and queer [LGBTQ] people). This involves evaluating current education in medical schools and residencies and developing training modules. Consequently, in addition to my work on researching and improving the health and well-being of LGBTQ individuals and communities, I've led many local and national initiatives with the American Medical Student Association and American Medical Association to incorporate additional training on LGBTQ health disparities and healthcare needs. At the end of the day, I never want anyone to feel the way I did long ago: alone and abandoned.

Nicole Danos

University of San Diego

I was born in Germany where I lived until I was seven, but my family always felt different from everyone else's. That's because we were Greek-Cypriot immigrants. We moved to Cyprus, where I started school...it turned out, I was different there, too! I spoke a second language, sometimes dressed funny (in traditional Bavarian outfits that my mom loved to dress me in), and really, really loved school. When I was twenty-one, I went to yet another country for college: the USA. Again, it took several years to feel like I could pass as a citizen, but this time I had a goal to become a marine biologist. I studied hard and eventually got my PhD studying how fish are built for swimming. I went to a new university, where I studied how leg muscles work in mammals. During that time, I became pregnant. That was such an exciting time! Not only would I become a mother, but I could observe my own body as it went through this fascinating transformation. I started reading up on what would happen to me and couldn't get enough. But I noticed something strange: there were not a lot of scientific studies available for me to learn from. There were especially very few studies about what would happen to my muscles. As I thought about everything I knew about pregnancy, I formed some hypotheses. Seven years have gone by since then, and I have two daughters and a research lab of my own. I now study what pregnancy does to leg muscles. I am also trying to build a baby bottle that looks more like a mother's real breast, because—guess what— we also don't know much about how breastfeeding works!

Michael A. Fisher

Federation of American Scientists

"Sure, whatever you say, Fish."

I still remember the bemused look on my friend's face, our class spread out around the tables in our elementary school library. We were all working on our reports that were due later that month, looking through piles of encyclopedias and books, gathering information for our papers. Our assignment for the day was to search the wood, metal, and paper card catalog for a word related to our topic, locate the spiny resources named on the cards on the shelves and shelves of books, page through and read the relevant information, write down the most important details—along with their sources—on index cards with our pencils, and repeat.

Libraries are special places. I become lost in them, engulfed by them. Books, recordings, music, magazines, newspapers, and movies roar with creativity, imagination, and knowledge of how the world works, beckoning to me, drawing me closer, wrapping me up into new worlds. I would bring home books like *The Andromeda Strain, Congo, Sphere,* and *Jurassic Park* by Michael Crichton, and *Fever, Outbreak,* and *Mutation* by Robin Cook, staying up way past my bedtime, reading with my sheets pulled up over my head, flashlight in my hand. I would picture myself in a lab coat, biohazard suit, or explorer's gear, discovering new medicines, studying a deadly virus, or adventuring into unknown territory with a team that I could count on.

Fascination turned into reality; I worked hard and became a scientist. With amazing teammates, I've built artificial proteins that enable microbes to live, engineered bacterial pumps to let out fuels, and found new ways to combat disease. Now, I help Congress learn about science and technology so that our country keeps getting stronger.

Kilan Ashad-Bishop

Breakthrough Miami

Kilan, who grew up in a house on a hill in Oakland, California, was a child fascinated by the world. She liked school so much, especially math, science, and reading, that she skipped first grade. For holidays, her family bought her rock collections and telescopes, which she liked much more than gifts like shoes and clothing. When her head was in a book, which was often, it was usually a Nancy Drew mystery novel. She was fascinated by the prospect of answering hard questions. When her head wasn't in a book, her feet were on the pavement. She was running around, picking up bugs, climbing trees, and exploring the world around her. She might have become an environmental scientist, but after losing her grandfather to heart complications, Kilan decided to become a scientist who solves biomedical mysteries and helps humans live healthier lives.

She went to college to study biology, then cancer biology. In graduate school, she conducted breast cancer research to design better treatments and improve outcomes for patients. In school, Kilan discovered that she was passionate about more than research and began to advocate for other things, such as policies to help students have more positive training experiences. She also regularly volunteered with black and brown girls who expressed interest in STEM, as they reminded her of her younger self. Though many of her mentors discouraged her from extracurricular activities, her passions beyond research only made her stronger. By the time she finished school, she was a published scientist and a fierce advocate for diversity and inclusion in education, science, and environmental justice. Now, Kilan merges her passions for problem solving and science, helping people come up with innovative solutions to a variety of problems, and trying to make the world a better place.

Wendy Suzuki

New York University

When Wendy Suzuki, a neuroscientist, started researching how the human brain—including her own—functions, it was a rough time for her. She had just joined a gym to lose the twenty-five pounds she gained during her initial years as a professor. This regular exercise (along with some serious carb monitoring) not only helped her get back in shape and lose weight, but also showed Wendy how much physical activity seemed to improve her mood and memory. In fact, exercising helped her with her studies and research focus in her own lab. This simple, accidental observation set off an avalanche of changes in Wendy's personal and professional life that included shifting her entire research program from the neurophysiology of memory in non-human primates to how physical aerobic exercise enhances brain function in humans. Wendy went on to write a book about that experience, give four TEDx talks, one 2017 TEDWomen talk, and countless other interviews and podcast recordings on the neuroscience of exercise in the human brain. In 2018, Wendy's TED Talk was the second most viewed talk, with 33 million viewers. Her book *Healthy Brain Happy Life* was made into a PBS special that has been shown all over the country.

Emily Balcetis

New York University

Emily found her way to psychology after earning a degree in classical and jazz music performance. She wanted to become a rock star, but was not well suited for that in a few ways. She achieved the height of her success when playing an outdoor festival for 15,000 people with a major punk and rock band. But that mark came too early in her career and was followed by too many performances with marching bands in plume-covered hats and polyester suits to give her any real street cred. So, she decided to study psychology at graduate school instead. In the first few months of her PhD studies, Emily planned a very undeserved summer break in Europe and was trying to find ways to fund her two-month trip. She designed a single study that coupled social psychology and visual perception with the hopes of presenting the data in a poster at a Vision Science conference in Glasgow and winning a $500 travel grant from Cornell to pay for the costs. The study worked, the graduate school awarded the grant, and off Emily went. Upon her return, her much too-accepting and open-minded graduate advisor suggested she conduct her research in consultation with the faculty at Cornell rather than in isolation and with only aspirations of one-off conference experiences—a suggestion that set her research on a much more challenging course. That single study defined the next twenty years of Emily's research agenda and founded what is now her comprehensive examination of the pervasiveness of motivational biases in conscious and unconscious visual perception and decision-making.

Joy Wolfram

Mayo Clinic

As an eleven-year-old, I took my dog Ronja to the veterinarian to treat a skin lesion. I watched in awe as skin swabs were seeded in petri dishes to see if Ronja had a bacterial infection. I asked the veterinarian if I could take some unused petri dishes home, but she objected. However, as I was about to leave, she handed me a bag and whispered, "Don't tell anyone." The same day, I started a miniature microbiology lab in my room, and my first experiment was swabbing our fridge. After a few days, the petri dishes were covered in different shapes and colors. I announced that our fridge was full of bacteria! My family was horrified. I realized that our fridge was not unusually dirty—science opens up new worlds that would otherwise go unnoticed. This experience triggered my initial interest in science.

Later, I witnessed many of my friends' parents pass away from cancer. I was frustrated that several decades of research had led to minor improvements in survival for certain types of aggressive cancers. I wanted to change the way we approach cancer research and decided to work with nanotechnology.

Amanda Spivey
Practicing dentist in Seattle

Ever since I can remember, even before kindergarten, I wanted a career where I could help people. I originally thought the best way to do this was by becoming a medical doctor, especially since I loved science. That was my plan up until one fateful Easter Sunday in seventh grade. I was out rollerblading in my neighborhood with my friends. One friend and I were playing a game, and unfortunately, I tripped over an uneven sidewalk and fell on my face. At the time I had orthodontic braces—there was blood everywhere. My lips were lacerated, teeth were chipped, chin was scraped—I was a mess. Luckily, I was not far from home. My mother picked me up and called my pediatric dentist. She graciously came in over the holiday weekend. She took a panoramic X-ray to check out the damage. I had fractured some teeth, broken part of my jaw, and cut up the inside of my mouth. Although the soft tissue injuries looked really bad, the braces had splinted my teeth together, so I did not end up knocking any of them out from the fall. My pediatric dentist reduced my jaw fracture and splinted my upper and lower teeth. She sutured my lip and reassured me and my frantic mother. After root canals, crowns, and fillings—and time—I was back on the mend. I also had a new appreciation for how much dentists could help change a patient's life. I continued on my science track through high school, became a pre-dental student in college, and went to dental school in Chicago. I now work as a general dentist with hospital and trauma training. My job lets me give back and properly treat people in situations like mine that Easter Sunday so many years ago.

About the Author

Faisal Hossain is a teacher who enjoys interacting with students at all levels and disciplines as part of his day job as a professor in the Department of Civil and Environmental Engineering at the University of Washington. His night job, to which he devotes an equal amount of energy, is about filmmaking and the communication of science. He uses these to build bridges between communities and solve pressing problems for society. His research group at the University of Washington focuses on improving quality of life in challenging environments through the application of science, technology, engineering, and math (STEM), with a focus on the supply of water, energy, and food. He initiated the Engineering Student Film Contest at the University of Washington in 2017, which is the nation's first and biannual student film festival for STEM majors as a way to explore the arts.

More information about his work can be found at WWW.SASWE.NET